A DK PUBLISHING BOOK

Project Editor Mary Atkinson
Art Editor Ivan Finnegan
Design Assistant Chris Drew
Deputy Managing Editor Dawn Sirett
Deputy Managing Art Editor
C. David Gillingwater
Production Josie Alabaster
US Editor Kristin Ward
Picture Research Joanne Beardwell
Photography Peter Anderson,
Dave King, and Gary Lewis
Illustrator Ellis Nadler

First American Edition, 1997
2 4 6 8 10 9 7 5 3 1

Published in the United States by
DK Publishing, Inc.,
95 Madison Avenue
New York, New York 10016
Visit us on the World Wide Web at http://www.dk.com

Color reproduction by Chromagraphics, Singapore
Printed and bound in Italy by L.E.G.O.

DK would like to thank the following for their
kind permission to reproduce photographs:
t=top, b=bottom, c=center, l=left, r=right

Bruce Coleman / C.B. & D.W. Frith 14-15c;
Frank Lane Picture Agency / Mark Newman 19br;
NHPA / Rich Kirchner 14bl; **Oxford Scientific Films** /
Animals Animals / Hans & Judy Beste 10bl, / Konrad Wothe
19tl; **Planet Earth Pictures** / Gary Bell 4cr, 8bl,
10-11c, / Peter J. Oxford 9br.

Scale
Look out for drawings
like this – they show
the size of the animals
compared with people.

Babirusa
Page 12

Marabou stork
Page 17

Crested porcupine
Page 20

Komodo dragon
Page 8

Tasmanian devil
Page 10

WEIRD CREATURES
OF THE WILD

Written by Theresa Greenaway

Ground hornbill
Page 16

Tapir
Page 6

Cassowary
Page 14

Guanaco
Page 18

Echidna
Page 21

Tapir

The strange-looking tapir lives in swampy rain forests. Its hefty body and short, strong legs are just the right shape to push through thick undergrowth.

🐾 The tapir's trunk is really an extra-long nose and top lip.

🐾 Tapirs leave piles of droppings as they move around to mark their territory.

🐾 A tapir can hide underwater. It uses its trunk just like a snorkel, poking it out to breathe.

Funny feet
Tapirs have unusual feet. They have four toes on each front foot, but only three on each hind foot.

Hoofed animals, such as tapirs, walk on their toes. A hoof is a large toenail that protects the toe bone.

🐾 An animal's **territory** is an area of land that it defends from others. 🐾

The Brazilian tapir's short, stiff mane helps protect its neck from overhanging branches.

The tapir has poor eyesight, but a good sense of smell. Nostrils at the tip of its trunk allow it to sniff out the tastiest roots and ripest shoots.

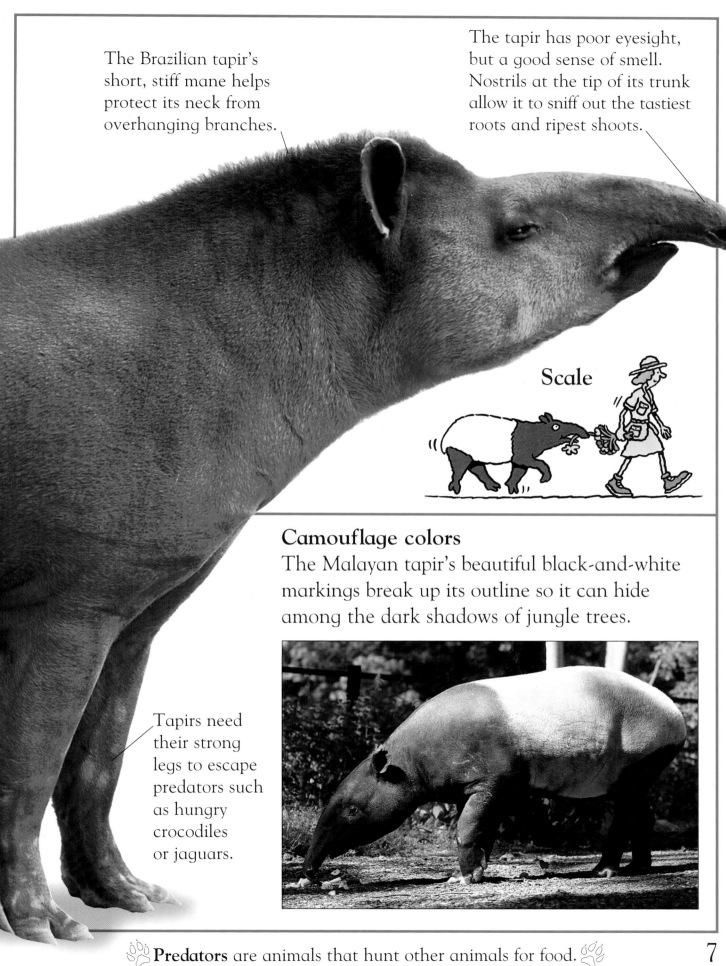

Scale

Camouflage colors
The Malayan tapir's beautiful black-and-white markings break up its outline so it can hide among the dark shadows of jungle trees.

Tapirs need their strong legs to escape predators such as hungry crocodiles or jaguars.

Predators are animals that hunt other animals for food.

Komodo dragon

🐾 A Komodo dragon can reach 10 ft (3 m) in length. That's one and a half times as long as your bed.

Komodo dragons are the world's largest lizards. They are found only on Indonesian islands, where they feed on goats, pigs, and deer – dead or alive! Sometimes they'll also attack unwary tourists.

Suitable suit
The Komodo dragon is covered in scales that protect it from sunburn and from becoming dehydrated.

🐾 When a Komodo dragon wants to keep another dragon away, it uses its long, powerful tail like a sword.

🐾 Komodo dragons group together to share large catches. However, the biggest lizards seize all the best pieces.

This Komodo dragon lives in a zoo. A special red lotion has been applied to its skin to keep it healthy.

Each toe on this giant lizard's feet ends in a long, sharp claw.

The Komodo dragon has ear openings on the sides of its head. It relies both on hearing and on sight to catch prey.

Cold-blooded hunter

Like all reptiles, Komodo dragons are cold-blooded. They need the sun's warmth for energy, but must not get too hot, so they hunt early in the day.

Scale

The Komodo dragon's tail is about the same length as the rest of its body.

Fast movers

Komodo dragons use their strong legs to chase prey. They can run fast over short distances, swim, and even climb low trees.

Cold-blooded animals depend on their surroundings for warmth.

Tasmanian devil

These fierce-looking creatures scavenge and hunt on the Australian island of Tasmania. They are called devils because of their spine-chilling screams.

This large, broad head supports very powerful jaw muscles.

Sharp, pointed teeth are for tearing meat.

Creatures of the night
At dusk, Tasmanian devils leave their daytime nests in hollow logs or rocky clefts to begin hunting.

Long whiskers help the Tasmanian devil feel its way when it's hunting at night.

Scale

When an animal searches for dead animals to eat, it is **scavenging**.

With their stocky bodies, these animals are suited mainly for scavenging or hunting slow prey.

Finger food
The Tasmanian devil is one of the few predators that uses its paws to push food into its mouth.

Thick fur keeps the Tasmanian devil warm even on cold winter nights.

AMAZING FACTS

A Tasmanian devil's strong jaws can crunch through the bones larger predators leave behind.

The Tasmanian devil has a huge appetite. It will eat everything from farmyard chickens to poisonous snakes.

The Tasmanian devil's short legs are ideal for foraging in dense undergrowth.

Like the kangaroo, the Tasmanian devil is a marsupial. A baby Tasmanian devil lives inside its mother's pouch until it is about fifteen weeks old.

A **marsupial** is an animal that is carried in its mother's pouch as a baby. 11

Babirusa

The babirusa is a type of wild pig from Indonesia. It lives in small family groups. A male babirusa has four incredible, curling tusks that keep growing until they almost touch his eyes.

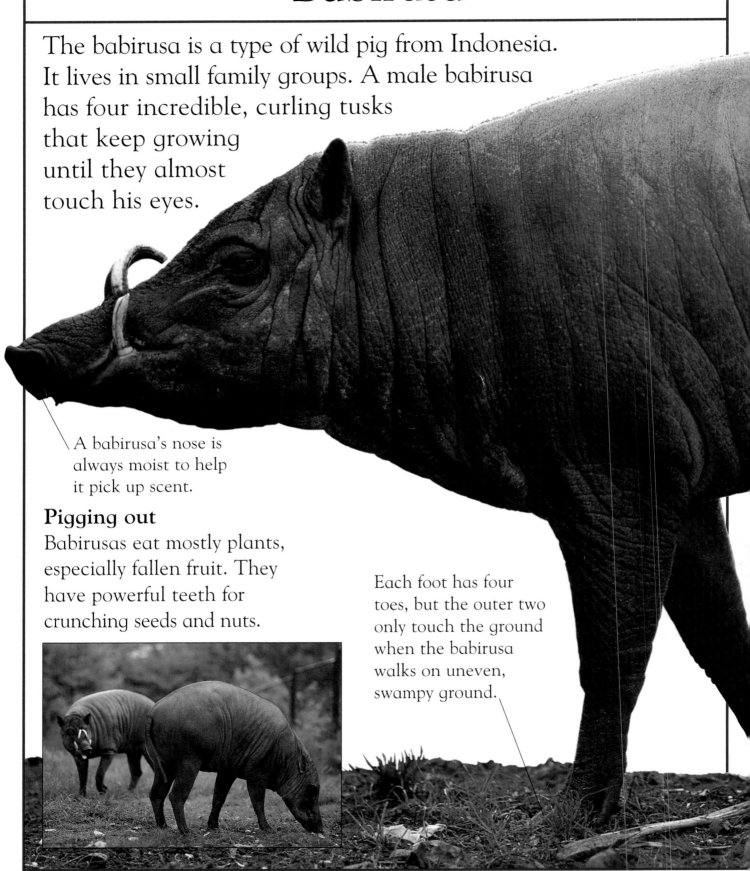

A babirusa's nose is always moist to help it pick up scent.

Pigging out

Babirusas eat mostly plants, especially fallen fruit. They have powerful teeth for crunching seeds and nuts.

Each foot has four toes, but the outer two only touch the ground when the babirusa walks on uneven, swampy ground.

Tusks are long teeth that can be seen even when an animal shuts its mouth.

Thick, protective skin hangs in folds and creases.

Brown-gray skin color matches the mud in which babirusas often wallow, helping them hide.

🐾 The tusks on most pigs poke out of their mouths. But, a male babirusa's two curly, upper tusks actually grow right through the skin on the top of his snout.

🐾 Males use their large curving tusks to show off to each other – and to attract female babirusas.

🐾 Unlike most other pigs, which have bodies covered in stiff bristles, the babirusa is almost completely hairless.

Scale

A fast getaway
The babirusa's long legs help it run quickly to escape predators, such as tigers.

🐾 To **wallow** in mud is to roll around in it. 🐾

Cassowary

A cassowary has a tall, bony casque on top of its head.

The cassowary may look comical, but it is actually one of the deadliest animals in Papua New Guinea. One kick from this bad-tempered bird can kill a person.

Both males and females have red, fleshy throat wattles.

The female lays up to eight eggs in a nest on the forest floor. The male then guards the eggs and keeps them warm.

Scale

A lonely life
Cassowaries are solitary birds, each one guarding its own territory. Males and females meet only to breed.

A **casque** is a hornlike bump that grows on top of a bird's beak and head.

Only adult cassowaries have these glossy black feathers. The young birds have brown feathers for camouflage.

No-one is quite sure why a cassowary has a casque on top of its head, but it may be a "crash helmet" for charging through dense brush.

During courtship, the bright blue skin on a male cassowary's neck swells up and quivers.

A cassowary can be up to 6 ft (1.8 m) tall. That's about the same height as a tall adult.

Thick skin protects a cassowary's legs from getting cut as it runs through tough undergrowth.

What big feet
The cassowary needs its wide-toed feet and strong legs to support its big, heavy body.

When threatened, a cassowary charges at its attacker, slashing out with its long, sharp claws on each inside toe.

Ground hornbill

Small troops of ground hornbills spend all day walking around the African savanna hunting for food. They keep in contact by making deep, booming calls. At night, they roost in trees or caves.

Both young and female Abyssinian ground hornbills have blue skin on their throats, while the adult males have pink skin.

A hornbill flies with slow, powerful beats of its large wings.

Scale

AMAZING FACTS

 Ground hornbills can walk up to 12 mi (19 km) in one day.

 Birds' casques and beaks are made of a similar material to your fingernails.

From scratch Ground hornbills find insects to eat by scratching at the ground with their sharp claws.

When on the ground, the hornbill uses its tail to help it balance.

When a bird **roosts**, it settles somewhere to sleep or rest.

Marabou stork

Using their long, pointed beaks like pickaxes, marabou storks clean up the remains of all kinds of African animals. These incredibly tall, fearless birds can even scare the vultures away from a carcass.

Scale

AMAZING FACTS

🐾 From head to toe, a marabou stork can measure 5 ft (1.5 m). That's about as high as the roof of a car.

🐾 From tip to tip, a marabou's wings can span up to 13 ft (4 m) – wider than two adult people lying head to toe.

Clean-cut bird
Even after a messy meal, these storks' bald heads are easy to keep clean.

Long legs help this stork stride through marshland.

Strong toes grip the branches of its night roost.

🐾 The remains and bones of a dead animal are called a **carcass**. 🐾 17

Guanaco

These hardy South American animals roam wild on the high slopes of the Andes mountains. Each small herd is guarded by a male, who bleats a loud alarm to warn of danger.

Scale

A narrow muzzle and a split upper lip allow the guanaco to nibble very short grass.

Mountain meals
Guanacos are herbivores. They graze on mountain grasses and wild plants.

An **herbivore** is an animal that mainly eats plants.

Bachelor group
When young males in the herd become adults, the older male leader chases them away. The young males then join up in groups.

On high mountains, there is less oxygen in the air. But guanacos cope better than we do. Their blood is especially good at taking in oxygen.

Guanacos raise and lower their short tails to send each other messages.

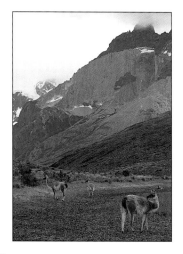

Cold-weather wear
Nights can be bitterly cold on the windy mountainsides. Guanacos need their thick, woolly coats to keep warm.

Like its relative, the camel, the guanaco only has two toes on each foot.

Some guanacos live up to 15,000 ft (4,500 m) above sea level. At this height, few trees can survive, only thick, tough mountain grasses.

Oxygen is a gas in the air that living things need in order to live.

Crested porcupine

When frightened, the African porcupine rattles its quills and stamps its feet. If this doesn't scare away a predator, the porcupine rushes backward, jabbing its long, sharp quills into its enemy.

Scale

A porcupine raises its quills to make itself look bigger when threatened.

Soft spot
A baby porcupine suckles milk near its mother's front legs – where it's not too prickly.

There are no quills on the face, just stiff bristles.

A porcupine's long, hollow spines are called **quills**.

Hollow, lightweight quills are not too heavy to carry around.

Echidna

This Australian marsupial is one of only three mammals to lay eggs. After the eggs hatch, the babies crawl into their mother's pouch. They stay there for up to ten weeks, growing bigger and stronger.

Scale

Nosy creature
The echidna uses its long snout to poke deep into crevices, sniffing out tasty ants and termites.

Short, sharp spines protect the echidna from predators, such as dogs.

Echidnas use the long claws on their hind feet to clean their spines.

The echidna's spines stick out through a layer of bristly hair.

🐾 When they are young, **mammals** suckle milk from their mothers. 🐾